From the heart

Susan Jones

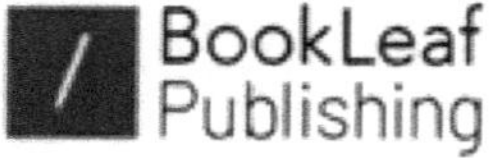

Presentation by *BookLeaf Publishing*

Web: www.bookleafpub.com

E-mail: info@bookleafpub.com

ISBN: 9789358736618

First edition 2022

DEDICATION

For my daughter Kimberley, with love

ACKNOWLEDGEMENT

I'd like to thank you the reader for taking time out of your day to relax and enjoy a little read, For the publication of my book big thanks go to bookleaf publishing for making my dream possible.
For my daughter who continues to support me and who told me to just go for it,xxxx

PREFACE

Hiya,my name is sue,I'm a 66 year old
grandmother who adores her daughter and
grandchildren, life hasnt always been easy,
I'm sure you will see from my poetry I write
from the heart,
I hope you enjoy reading as this is something
I've always wanted to do,
My love of poetry stems from reading as a child
I loved patience strong,
The humour of pam Ayers, and other poems.

Mermaid on the shore

I watched the changing waters
As it came closer to me.
I knew very soon
It would return me to the sea.
The very moment it reaches me
I will be gone from this place.
Taking with me a memory
Of your sweet smiling face.
We walked along the beach
Two lovers holding hands.
Explored every inch of the island
Made sweet love in the sand.
It was just by chance we met
You set out to do a chore.
I was sat all alone
At the very edge of the shore.
Waiting for my legs to take form you see
Then I may stand up and once again walk free.
You sat down beside me not much left to say
We talked of this and that then you helped me
get away.
You never knew the change I had gone through
Right before your eyes I turned into something
new.
I had been spellbound to swim the oceans deep
Once every few years allowed to take this leap.

I've experienced so much just being with you
My time on the shore has ended now but I know
what to do.
For true love to finally break this spell
The zea must reclaim me and drag me back to
hell.
Now I've paid my Price I'll be alone no more
I will return to you my sweetheart
As you wait along the shore.

She looked at me.

She looked at me ,with eyes ,that couldn't
understand,
All she did was reach out
I gently took her hand.
I tried to reassure her,
She would be alright.
I often had to go to her
In the middle of the night.
The world around her grew strange,
She just didn't comprehend,
A part of her mind was gone forever,
It could never mend.
Most of her life she couldn't remember ,
I was there to help her
With words so tender,
With gentle persuasion and loads of love ,
The only way I seemed to get through
She was lost in her own world ,
She just didn't know what to do.

She looked at me with eyes that didn't
understand,
Why the woman she called nurse,
Was attending to her demands.
All she did was garbled,

In words that didn't make sense,
Like , "put the kettle on me fire, I have to kick
the garden fence ".

She looked at me with eyes that didn't
understand,
All I could do was teach her,
Help her, be patient with her, hold her hand.
It wasnt her fault,
She doesn't know what to do,
She was lost in her own mind
I just couldn't get through.

She was my mom, my darling, my friend.
I loved her and continued nursing her,
Until her lifes end.
Alzheimer's was a cruel trick to play,
It took my beautiful mom away
I will love and miss her always xxx

Driftwood

It was just a piece of driftwood
Lying there on the beach.
Quite where it came from I could say,
It seemed to have travelled a very long way.
It must have once stood proud, strong and free,
In someone's garden,this magnificent tree.
Lovers carved their names in the bark ,
Lanterns hung from its branches when it got
dark.
A child once had a swing
From one of the trees sturdy limbs.
A beautiful treehouse was built.
It housed many different things,
The years flew past,parts withered and died,
When a raging storm with high winds,
Tore the tree from it's very roots,
You could almost hear it cried.
The storm raged ,on and on.
When morning came,the tree was gone.
Hour after hour, day after day,
Out at sea it bobbed,as it was taken away,
Parts broke off,the once proud tree was no more
All that was left was what was washed up on the
shore.
This magnificent tree,so gentle, so mild,wound
up beached,

Then along came a child,

His daddy took one look and suddenly he knew,
He couldn't believe what he was about to do,
Although the child was only three,
He hadn't spoken a word until he saw the tree,
Not once in his three young years.
Daddy couldn't hold back the tears.

He dragged, he pulled, he pushed, he shoved,
eventually, the driftwood budged.
Daddy made it back home.
Driftwood now had a permanent place.
He watched his young son as a huge smile
spread across his face.
It's as though the driftwood had finally reached a
part,
Hidden deep inside this sweet young boys heart,
Now you couldn't stop the chatter,
He played, he laughed, he smiled,
So now it didn't matter,
Three years ago when he lost his wife
His son never spoke a word,he thought his boy
was dumb,
Now the tree had given him the power of
speech,
It was the sweetest moment he could ever hope
to reach.

Twilight time

To all you lovers and dreamers too,
It's twilight time,
Here's a special one just for you.
When your falling asleep,
You conjure up a face,
Their smile, their eyes.
There's no time or space,
The image becoming, oh,so clear
You wish with all your heart,you could hold
them near.
Wherever they are,
Whatever they do
In twilight they will think of you,
They may not know what you say,
They think about you, night and day
Dreams can become real, through the passing of
time,
It's what you both feel,
Eventually your souls entwine,
It's twilight your love becomes devine.

New life

You hold a new life in your hand ,
You hope and you pray things turn out well .
You marvelled at your tummy,as you watched it
swell.
You felt each and every kick,all the movements
inside,
Along with mixed emotions, filling you up with
pride.
Then comes the long awaited day,
It's finally here,
Now your elated, yet also full of fear ,.
You created a new life,
You hold her gently, she won't break.
As you get used to her .
Your bound to make mistakes.
She looks to you,your mouth is struck dumb.
She's beautiful, just perfect,
Your proud to be her mom.

For my amazing daughter Kimberley xxxx

Take that first step

Taking that first step,is always the hardest ,
Just take a deep breath, and try.
I know things dont look possible.
You not going to suddenly sprout wings and fly.
Each step you take,though it may seem hard at
first.
Once you take the first one,
Then your over the worst.
You can do it.
Your heart is strong,
Its beating inside you,
You wont go wrong.
You make a decision, you can see it through,
Take whatever comes, it's really up to you.
Dont be afraid, to show that you care.
You never know that special someone,
Could be waiting out there.
Watching, waiting, to see what you do.
The world is your oyster,
Take that first step, make your dreams come
true.

Empty chair.

Sometimes I see the empty chair,
I picture you sitting there.
The memories come flooding back.
It was so very hard to let you go,
My heart wasn't ready.
Yet the more I tried,I knew it was too late.
After all you were the one in pain,
I couldn't see you suffering, you couldn't take
the strain.
We visited you in hospital,
I bought mom along too.
Although her mind couldn't comprehend,
Your body was turning blue.
I see your image so vividly,
I knew I had to take mom away.
Then came the dreaded phone call,
You passed away later that day.
I cherish your memory.
You meant the world to me,
When mom passed to join you,
It set your spirits free.
You never were a burden,
Dad ,I loved you so.
I think about you often
I just wanted you to know.

You sleep with the Angel's.
Mom is by your side.
Together for eternity, she was your ever loving
bride.
God bless you both,
Miss you everyday,
So thinking about you
This poem I wrote to say,
Love you mom and dad,,
Always your loving daughter sue xxxxx

Her mask

She wears her mask with dignity,
It stands out from the crowd.
She doesn't care what people think
She hears their thoughts out loud,
Their snide little gestures,
Their false silly smiles.
She's a woman with a past,so what !
Not everyone who judges knows,
They all have something that hurt,in a small
way.
Maybe a slight remark, a nudge or a wink ,
Let them carry on,
She doesn't care what people think .
She's tired of the games people play,
This time she's doing her own thing,
In her own unique way.
Let them do or say what they want,
She won her freedom to choose.
It took a while to make up her mind,
Now she has nothing to loose.
She wears her mask with dignity,
She no longer gives a jot,
If people don't like what they see,
Then they can go and trot..

He came to claim my soul today

He came to claim my soul today
He'd been waiting a long long time.
I'd make him wait much longer ,but,
I had to answer one day for my crime.

I was a star struck starlet,
Got in with my looks and charm,
I'd turned many a head,with just one glance
Yet I'd never do any harm,(or so I thought)

The producer of the play,
Maximilian was his name,
Went through a list of actors and actresses.
It was more like a who's who,
When he looked straight across at me,
I knew what I had to do.

I wanted him to cast me
In whatever role he had,
I didn't care what part it was,
I could be demure or seductively bad.

Fortune must have smiled on me .

He chose me, I got the part.
I'd act my flipping heart out.

IT certainly was a great start
Rave reviews followed
A new star was born,
My pact with the devil worked so well
People were hooked on my charm.

I went to exotic places,
Dined with the crem de la crem
Champagne and caviar for breakfast
Fans flocked to be near this fem.

He came to claim my soul today.
For all the world to see,
The producer drank a lethal potion,
Concocted of course by me,

I sipped the same napoleon brandy, but
I never got my lips wet.
In his I'd added the potion,
Strangely enough, acquired from my handsome
vet.

He'd left me an absolute fortune,
When the will read.
I played my part so convincingly,
As I tended him on his death bed.

Many years I was his mistress.
Now that was about to change,

My epitaph will read.
She beat him at his own game.

He came to claim my soul today.
I really didn't care.
I'd had the last laugh,
As I was placed in the coffin,
The actress they knew
Wasn't really there....

Medusa

Listen, do you want to know a secret.
Do you promise not to tell.
Come closer,let me whisper in your ear.
Why do you tremble and shake with fear.
I medusa, wouldn't hurt you my dear.
Listen, I need to go away.
Just for a break, a little holiday.
"Can you do something for me,
My snakes ,they are attached to my head."
"Could you do this for me, they need to be fed,"
"You can do this,wont you agree,"
Come closer I need to tell you one more thing .
"Just be very careful of there sting".
I know it is indeed a great big task.
But you see I have no one else to ask.,
" Its fine,I will do this for you "I said,
"So long as you consider not biting off my
head".

The vicar

"Get yer filthy paws
Off me silky drawers",
The woman said to the vicar.
I ad t turn and walk away,
It didn't arf make me snicker.
She had tucked er dress into er pants,
A funny sight t see,
'Cause I remember doing the same,
Yeah, once it happened t me.
"Don't look at me ,in that tone of voice,
Yer smell a funny colour,".
Was summat else she said to im,
When he grabbed her arm to pull er.
Poor vicar,he just crossed his self,
Then slowly, walked away.
Off she trots,she's cussing.
"Wots the world coming to t day.

Me granddad's teeth

"I like to suck cock".
Me grandad was heard to say.
He's got a bag of rock
I gave him,just today,
But he went and took his teeth out,
That's why he sounds that way.

"Me bums really sore,
Put some cream on it chuck".
What he means is his gums,
He don't seem to be having much luck.
I wish he would put his teeth back in,
'Cause everyone can hear him,
It's making them grin.
Bless him ,he cant eat with his teeth.

Aunt florries forgetfulness

Aunt florries forgetfulness
Gets me in a state,
I called on her today,
She left open the garden gate.
I walked into her kitchen,
Just in time to see,
She's sat there cuddling her slipper,
Trying to feed it tit bits.

She suddenly looks at me and said,
"Me cats got a bad tummy",
"I think me cats off colour a bit"
Oh, she did look funny .

"I've come to make your dinner ",I said,
With a sigh ,she pushed her slipper away.
"I think me poor cat is dead".

Well I didn't know what to say.
Just in time, in walks her cat,
He sauntered into the room.
Up she gets from her seat,
Trying to chase her slipper away with her
broom.

Auntie florries forgetfulness
Sometimes makes my day,
She's a dear old soul and,
I wouldn't have her any other way.

The window cleaner

Sometimes life just ups,
And smacks you in the face.
Take this morning for instance,
Having a shower is no disgrace.
Except when I forgot,
It's the window cleaners day.
There I am with my bits on show,
Much to my dismay.
I forgot to close the blinds,
Not much that I could do.
Yet that's not the worse part,
My shower curtains are see through.

I quickly grab a towel,
Dash for cover in my bedroom,
Only to find he's moved his ladder,.
I really could have swooned.

Hastily, I get dressed,
My hair still soaking wet,
As I dash downstairs to pay him,
Bugger it,how could I forget.

I'm wearing a white blouse .
My hair is dripping wet.

The window cleaner, winked at me,
He's got a flipping cheek,
He said, "didn't recognise you with your clothes
on,
Bye, see you again in 3 weeks.

Baby at the zoo

Hello all, how's this for a laugh.
Have you ever seen a baby,
Try to kiss a giraffe.
It's long neck bent down,
Baby took a look.
IT was just in that moment,
Yes,that's all it took,
Out came his tongue,
All wet with spit.
You can probably guess, the very next bit.
Baby's face , got a very wet lick.
I promise it's true,
'Cause my camera went click.
Yet in my haste,
Guess what I did.
I forgot to remove
The flipping camera lens lid.

The old puppeteer

Ever since she was a young girl
Her marionettes she would use.
Everywhere she went ,people stopped to look,
You just couldn't refuse.

They came from miles around,
To see her and watch them dance.
They were so very lifelike,
You were held spellbound, locked in a trance.

She had an old lady puppet,
Who got up to do a jig,
Dancing along the park pathways,
The marionette wasn't very big.

The old lady who controls her,
Made her captive audience laugh.
Children used to squeal with delight,
As they posed for a photograph.

The marionette fed the squirrels,
She carried a small bag of nuts.
In her tiny hands they trusted her,
She posed no threat today,

Birds would flock around her ,
To see the marionette play.

Made now in her own image,
She resembled her,
Even the clothes she wore.
With her tiny shoes and her walking stick,
She dragged along the floor.

As with the passage of time,
She grew older, as did her marionette.
The puppeteer with her little bag of nuts,
Her marionette was the best yet.

Fairy in the garden

Ssshhh,be very quiet,
Watch out where you put your feet,
For there at the bottom of the garden is,
A fairy ,fast asleep.

Please do not wake her,
She had a very busy night.
Learning all sorts of fairy things.
Trying hard to get them right.

She flew around the gardens
Making every thing just neat,
When she came upon this resting place,
Now doesn't she look so sweet.

Ssshhh, don't wake her,
Let her sleep a little while,
For come the morning when her work is done,
You can look at your garden and smile.

All the winter flowers,
Standing so majestic.
Everything is beautiful,
Looking quite fantastic.

Let the poor girl sleep.
She's really earned her wings.
You can tell she's done a good job
Because all the birds just sing.

Escapees

In the graveyard
Where all souls lie,
I was mesmerised by the sight
As I was passing by.

The devil took a damsel
Right there on a graveyard bench.
I was frozen, stood transfixed,
She looked a comely wench.

With his huge talons
He tore her sateen dress.
Blood dripping from her,
She didn't sound in distress.

Her tongue came out,
She licked her lips,
Then slowly opening her thighs,
The devil then took her
Right before my eyes.

Next minute, the sirens blew,
Police were everywhere.
I stood watching what they would do,
They placed them in straight jackets,

Carted them both away.
They had escaped from the asylum, on a fancy
dress costume day.

Christmas in our house

Christmas in our house,
In the years past.
" how many sleeps now mom,
'Til Santa's here at last".?

The gorgeous aroma of cooking, yum yum.
Makes my tastebuds go AWOL,
rumbling noises in my tum.

Dad worked extra hard ,
Always to and fro,
Then rushing upstairs to hide presents
So we didn't know.

Mom got extra wool.
She would knit dollys clothes,
With beautiful bonnets, all ribbons and bows.
One doll in particular, I can still recall,
In a new knitted outfit,
Dressed ready for a ball.

Paper chains we all made to hang from the
ceiling,
Longer and longer ,the living room was
streaming.

A big coal fire, bucket and logs all ready,
Mom's knitting needles clacking,
Finishing off a teddy.

Dad's brylcreem hair, all nice and slick,
Shining to tame his locks so thick.
His fair isle jumper in Christmas green,
Mom had knitted it one year ,
Was a sight to be seen.

Christmas morning, awake with the lark,
Dad stumbles downstairs, still outside it's dark.
Fire needed stoking,
More coal with a big log.
An extra bone in the bowl for jacey our dog.

Eyes wide open, a Christmas sight to see,
All the amount of presents under the Christmas
tree.
Mom and dad's faces,all aglow,
Ours was a happy home ,long long ago.

Neighbours shouting "merry Christmas ",
Over the garden fence.
Mom handing out mince pies ,
She made late last night.
Her face and hands covered in flour,
A very memorable sight.

I look back now to see,two empty chairs,
Our Christmases were magical,
I send them love in my prayers,
Merry Christmas mom and dad ,
Up in heaven above,
We love you and we miss you,
This comes with our undying love,
For joan and john Cummings. (our beautiful
parents)
From your twins ,,susan and Richard. Xxxx

Remembering you

In the stillness of the night
When the world is fast asleep,
Into my mind ,you often creep.
 A fleeting image I see of you,
Reminding me of a love
So pure, so true.
Of innocence,
Before the world made it change,
That fateful night so long ago,
A stormy sea,a blizzard,
A gigantic wave.
I see it now ,
The vision I can't erase.
Water washed over the boat,
Coughing, spluttering,
I nearly choked.
Hands reaching down,
Pulling this way and that
Far out at sea ,I saw bobbing up and down
Your silly little hat.

I'm on the shoreline, I'm safe and sound,
Debris is lying everywhere,
You were nowhere to be found.

I often saw you gazing, out across the sea,
A tear escaping,
Are you still looking for me?

I'm safe mommy, please dont cry no more,
Look up to the night sky,
Like you used to do before.
Blazing across, a shooting star,
See mommy,I'm here,
I didn't go far.
You will always hold me,
Locked in your heart.
Goodnight mommy darling,
Love your little sweetheart

A vow of love

I want to hold your hand
For the rest of my life,
I cherish the day,you first became my wife.
We have seen many things ,
In our lives together.
We had our ups and downs,
We faced them whatever.
I never want to lose you,
So let me be the first to go,
I will wait for you in heaven,
At the gates,just to to show,
Life with you has been magical,
I never want it to end.
Your my partner, my soul mate,
My sweetheart, my friend.
The day I set eyes on you ,
I already knew,
That I would spend eternity,
To never make you feel blue.
You gave me a ring,
The day that we wed.
I showered you with kisses
That night in our wedding bed.
You stole my heart.
You will be forever with me,
I made a vow of love,
For eternity.